How to Look Good on Paper.

by Haller Schwarz

D0972795

A PERIGEE BOOK

Turning English into an effective language for business was a thankless job strewn with misplaced prepositions, passive verbs and irrelevant adjectives. But someone had to do it. Who but Haller Schwarz? A leading advertising agency in business-to-business communications. A 25-year veteran of the information wars. A noted crusader against corporate biz-speak. And the first black belt in boardroom linguistics.

How to Look Good on Paper is illustrated by Dick Chodkowski and written by Hank Schwarz.

Perigee Books
are published by
The Putnam Publishing Group
200 Madison Avenue
New York, NY 10016

First Perigee Edition 1988

Library of Congress Cataloging-in-Publication Data

Haller Schwarz.
   How to look good on paper.

   Bibliography: p.
   1. Business writing.   2. English language—Business
English.   I. Title.
HF5718.3.S32   1988   808'.066651   88-5837
ISBN 0-399-51481-3

Printed in the United States of America

1   2   3   4   5   6   7   8   9   10

To Friends
Who Have Made Us
Look Good.

Good business writing starts with good organization. Here's where business gets organized.

Contents.

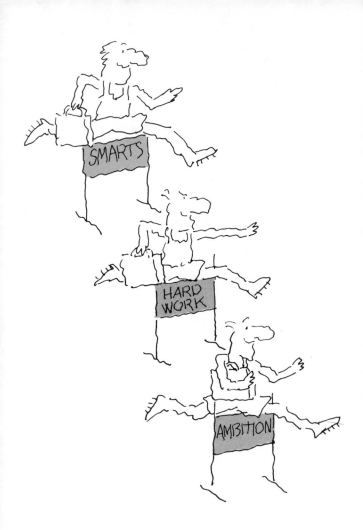

There is an unwritten law in the business world.

You are what you write.

What makes good business writing so important?

1. Good writing saves you time. It actually helps you write faster and easier.

2. Good writing makes you look professional.

3. Good writing gets *results.*

This book reviews good business writing. Read it through now, and keep it handy when you write. You'll be surprised how quickly your business letters, memos and reports get easier to write and easier to read.

In fact, you won't believe how good you' ll look on paper.

How to mean business when you write.

How to mean business when you write.

20 basic strategies to help you say what you mean.

Successful writers should lead their associates out of confusion, not into it.

Start by following these 20 practical rules, and you'll make it easier for everyone to follow you.

1. Get to the point.

Write so busy people can read and understand your writing quickly. The purpose of any document you write should be clear from the start.

2. Say it clearly the first time.

Make your communication complete. Include everything the reader needs to know.

Say it all clearly now so you won't have to say it again later.

3. Plan ahead.

Think before you write. Collect and organize the facts before you begin.

4. Keep it short and simple.

Make your writing easy to read. Use short sentences and paragraphs. Most readers prefer sentences of 18 words or less, and paragraphs of not more than six or eight lines.

5. Be emphatic.

Place important information first or last for emphasis. *Underline sentences.* Number the points you wish to make.

> Put main thoughts
> in indented paragraphs.

And now the bad news—put negative information in the middle of paragraphs to de-emphasize it.

6. Break it up.

Look for ways to break up long paragraphs and sentences. List main ideas for easy reading. Break long sentences into several shorter sentences, using conjunctions such as *and, but* and *or.*

Hard: There are numerous reasons why the London Conference failed, many of which, of course, you already know.

Easier: The London Conference failed for several important reasons, but many of these you already know.

7. Don't connect what doesn't connect.

Don't join two sentences containing ideas that have no clear relationship. The resulting sentence won't make very much sense.

Example: We know we can find the source of the error,   (independent)

and the new machines work.
(independent)

8. Commas aren't connectives.

Don't use a comma alone to join two independent sentences. Use a comma and a connective word.

Wrong: We know we can find the source of the error,   (independent)

we have all the records.
(independent)

Right: We know we can find the source of the error,   (independent)

for we have all the records.
(independent)

9. Write complete sentences.

Don't separate related groups of words—phrases or clauses—from the sentences to which they belong. Write complete sentences.

Wrong: We can correct the ledger by Tuesday. If we can find the error.

Right: We can correct the ledger by Tuesday if we can find the error.

*Your writing is often the first impression
others have of you. Make it a good one.*

10. Spell it right.

Check the dictionary or a spelling guide when you're
unsure about the spelling of a word. Keep a running
list of the words you misspell and refer to it. A list of
commonly misspelled words can be found on page 48.
Try to memorize their correct spelling.

11. Keep it together.

Don't separate a modifier—a word, phrase or clause that limits or explains another word, phrase or clause—from the word it modifies. Keep them as close together as possible.

Confusing: The secretary had her typewriter on the desk which she had purchased from IBM.

Which did she purchase from IBM?

Clear: The secretary had her typewriter, which she had purchased from IBM, on her desk.

12. Wake it up.

Make your writing interesting and lively. Use *present* tense and *active* verbs. Use personal pronouns. Example—use "we" and "you" instead of "lessor" and "lessee." Vary sentence length. Use complex sentences to express cause-effect relationships.

13. Be accurate.

An inaccurate communication implies that you are either careless or incompetent.

Know the subject you're writing about *before* you begin. Look up the facts first, *then* write.

Errors in business can be expensive. Promises and acknowledgments can be legally binding.

Trim verbal deadwood.
You'll never miss it.

14. Eliminate deadwood.

Some words and expressions take up space but don't add meaning. Try to condense unimportant ideas. Business writing should be as brief as possible. Omit unnecessary adverbs—words that end in *-ly*.

Not:	Hopefully, I will see you soon.
But:	I hope to see you soon.

15. Be clear.

Organize for clarity. If you limit each paragraph to one subject, your paragraphs will be short and easy to read. Begin with the central idea; then give details.

Group things that are alike, and separate unrelated ideas. Use an outline to help you organize your thoughts.

16. Revise your work.

Proofread your writing to clarify ideas, to eliminate clutter and to catch errors.

Keep your tone conversational. Talk to the reader as if he were in the room.

17. Make it easy on the reader.

Construct sentences that are easy to understand. If a sentence has to be reread, it is poorly worded. Simple, direct sentences save time for the busy reader and the busy writer.

Don't waste your reader's time – write sentences that get to the point.

18. Keep your references clear.

Be sure to make a pronoun's antecedent clear. An antecedent is the word to which a pronoun refers.

Confusing: Joe sent the memo to Bob just before he was promoted.

               Who was promoted – Joe or Bob?

Clear: Just before Joe was promoted, he sent the memo to Bob.

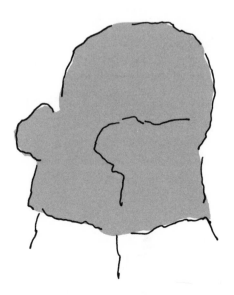

19. Don't bump.

Move smoothly from one paragraph to another by using transitional expressions. (Use the list on page 76.)

20. Be conversational.

Write in words that your reader will be familiar with and understand. The simple word is preferred in business. Use words of three syllables or less.

Know your basics: letters, memos and reports.

Know your basics: letters, memos and reports.

When to write which; how to write each.

Letters, memos and reports hold businesses together. So it's smart to stick to some rules.

Let's start with letters.

1. Letter perfect.

Study the good business letters that come to you, and you'll soon notice a few things. First, they all share that basic structure—that's why they're letters.

Every letter, in fact, has three distinctive parts. Here are a few things you should know about each.

THE OPENING.

The opening should be specific, personal and positive:

1. Make the opening short.

2. Get to the point; let your reader understand the purpose of the letter immediately.

3. If you are asking for something, ask for it here.

4. Put good news in the first sentence when the letter carries good news.

5. Begin with a "thank you" when the letter carries disappointing news.

6. Identify clearly the subject of the letter.

7. Don't use cliches at the beginning of a letter— avoid pointless or dull openings.

THE BODY.

1. Develop details in the body of the letter.

2. Construct each paragraph around one central point.

3. Make your points so that they can be understood.

THE CLOSE.

1. Close with an action statement.

2. Try to suggest only one action—and set a deadline.

3. If it is appropriate, ask for recommendations.

Eight instant ways to make any letter better.

1. *Plan your letters.* Determine the purpose of the letter before you write.

2. *Create goodwill.* Whether you bear good news or bad, you want the customer to remain loyal and to increase his patronage.

3. *Create a positive tone.*

• *Be prompt.* All the writing skill in the world won't keep a customer whose letter has gone unanswered for a long time.

• *Be straightforward.* If your reader understands, he or she will be more likely to trust you and to react positively.

• *Choose your words carefully.* Be business-like, but sincere and friendly—not overly formal.

The best business letters have a friendly, conversational tone.

Remember that your writing is intended for people.

4. *Personalize your letters.* Adapt them to your reader, and write from his point of view.

Make it clear to your readers that you are thinking of them—use their names whenever appropriate.

5. *Be courteous.* Show respect for the reader's intelligence and integrity.

A sarcastic or accusing letter discredits the writer and the business he represents.

A good way to show courtesy is to stress "you" rather than "I" or "we."

6. *Use the active voice to make your writing lively.*
Example: Henry sent a memo.

7. *Use the passive voice to de-emphasize who's doing what.*
Example: A memo was sent by Henry.

8. *Be positive.* Avoid negative words and accusations.

Not: We cannot approve your budget
          request for more than $15,000.

But: We can approve your budget request
          for up to $15,000.

Greetings and salutations.

Every business letter starts with some kind of salutation.

Depending on who will read your hello, you can say it in several ways.

1. *One Person – Name, Gender, and Courtesy Title Preference Known*

   Dear Mr. (Mrs., Ms., Miss) Wells:

2. *One Person – Name Known, Gender Unknown*

   Dear Pat Hartman:

   Dear P. G. Hartman:

3. *One Woman – Courtesy Title Preference Unknown*

   Dear Ms. Smith:

   Dear Sarah Smith:

4. *Two or More Men*

   Dear Mr. Jones and Mr. Harris:

   Gentlemen:

   Dear Messrs. Jones and Harris:

5. *Two or More Women*

   Individual – Dear Mrs. Sharp, Ms. Smith, and Miss Harris:

Individual – Dear Mrs. Jordan and Mrs. Kent:
Combined – Dear Mesdames Jordan and Kent:
Individual – Dear Ms. Jordan and Mrs. Kent:
Combined – Dear Mses. (Mss.) Jordan and Kent:
Individual – Dear Miss Jordan and Miss Kent:
Combined – Dear Misses Jordan and Kent:

6. *A Woman and a Man*
   Dear Ms. Sharp and Mr. Jordan:

7. *Several Persons*
   Dear Mrs. Hall, Miss White, Mr. Gomez,
      and Mrs. Green:
   Dear Friends (Colleagues, Members, etc.):

8. *An Organization Composed Entirely of Men*
   Gentlemen:

9. *An Organization Composed Entirely of Women*
   Mesdames:
   Ladies:

10. *An Organization Composed of Men and Women*
    Gentlemen:
    Ladies and Gentlemen:
    Dear James Smith: (Head of Organization)
    Dear Sir (Madam): (Head of Organization;
                        Name and Gender Unknown)

26

Messrs. | Mses. | Friends

How-to-answer-a-complaint dept.

1. Be courteous, dignified and fair.

2. Don't accuse.

3. Don't make threats or demands.

4. Suggest reasonable adjustments.

5. Be sure of the facts.

6. State clearly the cause of the complaint.

7. Show the resulting inconvenience or loss.

8. Appeal to the recipient's sense of honesty and fairness.

Apologies and other bad news.

1. Admit the error immediately and explain. (If you fear such an admission may have legal implications, check with the Legal Department first.)

2. Promptly send your apology, before bad feelings have time to grow.

3. End on a positive note—the give-us-another-chance theme.

4. Don't exaggerate your error.

LETTERS THAT CARRY DISAPPOINTING NEWS.

1. Express appreciation for something.

2. Give a logical explanation and be sympathetic.

3. Offer alternatives.

4. Change the subject as quickly as possible.

5. State your desire to deliver a requested service before delivering the unpleasant news that you can't.

6. Don't slam the door—remember that the customer or former customer is still a prospect for a different service or the same service at a later date.

Letters of confirmation.

1. Confirm in writing any important oral agreements.

2. Clarify issues, agreements, or details.

3. Establish responsibilities.

4. Clearly state your purpose.

5. Invite a response if you anticipate disagreement.

6. Be *specific* about who is to do what, where, and when.

Not: Please sign and return the enclosed form as soon as possible.

But: Please sign and return the enclosed form before January 5, 2001.

7. Don't use dull, formal closings. Don't use a participle (a word that ends in -*ing*) to end a letter.

Not: Thanking you in advance, I remain.

But: Thank you for your cooperation.

Be prompt. The best writing in the world won't make up for a late reply.

Acknowledgments and replies to inquiries.

1. Express appreciation for the request or inquiry.

2. Acknowledge every request.

3. Redirect to the proper office inquiries you can't answer. If the letter was not originally addressed to you, explain why you are answering.

4. If fulfillment of the request is not possible, explain why.

5. Be helpful. Suggest other sources if you can't help, and provide additional information if it is relevant.

6. Offer further help.

Heartwarming form letters.

Many hours can be saved when you develop a good standardized form letter.

If you are writing the same basic letter to a number of individuals or businesses, let the Word Processing Department help you.

SUGGESTIONS FOR DRAFTING FORM AND GUIDE LETTERS.

1. Collect copies of letters on the same subject.

2. Note the similarities and differences in the letters. Also note the sentences and paragraphs that are repeated; choose the best from these.

3. Make an outline of all the points to be covered.

4. Draft a sample letter and submit it for approval.

5. Frequently revise form letters—they rapidly become outdated.

2. Memos: the less said, the better.

A memo is sometimes called an "internal letter." A memo saves time and money when you are writing to people within your organization.

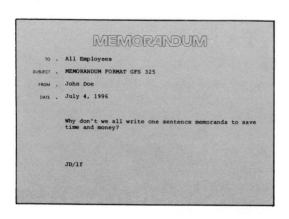

MEMORANDUM

TO . All Employees

SUBJECT . MEMORANDUM FORMAT GFS 325

FROM . John Doe

DATE . July 4, 1996

Why don't we all write one sentence memoranda to save time and money?

JD/lf

Accuracy, clarity, and brevity are ''memo musts.''

1. Use abbreviations.

2. Confine a memo to one subject.

3. Write a memo in outline form when it is convenient. Be sure the outline is clear and easy to understand.

4. State the purpose of the memo in the first sentence.

5. State future action that is to be taken.

A major advantage of a memo is that it will give you written documentation. Sometimes, however, it is easier, faster, and less expensive to telephone rather than write—especially to a fellow employee.

3. Reports: why, what and how.

Informal Reports and Report Memos contain three main elements:

    (1) a statement of purpose,

    (2) a message, and

    (3) a statement of future action to be taken.

Simply stated—WHY, WHAT, HOW.

PURPOSE.

A report should convey facts about a particular subject.

STYLE.

1. An impersonal style is usually used in reports— evaluations should be based on facts and sound reasons rather than on hunches or opinions. Reasoning from facts is important to the success of any business report.

2. A report should be as brief as possible. Say everything that needs to be said in the fewest words necessary.

ORGANIZATION.

1. Use the format that you believe is best suited to your reader and your material.

2. An organized report carries the reader smoothly from one idea to another. Arrange facts in logical units and sequences.

*Business is already drowning in paperwork.
Make sure a report is necessary before
adding to the deluge.*

33

COMPANY GROWTH: THE PAST TEN YEARS

Purpose

This report presents an overview of the Company's
substantial growth during the past decade. This paper
should help management to make decisions regarding the
company's future.

A Decade of Phenomenal Growth

Sales growth provides the best measure of the
Company's performance over the past ten years. The
following chart lists our increasing annual sales:

-Fiscal year 1	$1,063,673,397
-Fiscal year 2	$1,137,512,928
-Fiscal year 3	$1,369,927,335
-Fiscal year 4	$1,632,930,031
-Fiscal year 5	$1,788,472,458
-Fiscal year 6	$1,928,665,037
-Fiscal year 7	$2,206,047,350
-Fiscal year 8	$2,687,611,456
-Fiscal year 9	$3,186,084,697
-Fiscal year 10	$3,776,157,026

These figures indicate that we have grown very
quickly.

The Factors Responsible for the Past Decade's Growth

Four factors have played principal roles in the
Company's growth. These factors are:

1. The introduction of new customer services to meet
   changing customer needs.
2. Dedication to community service.
3. Friendly and efficient personnel.
4. Aggressive management.

Summary

In the past decade, the Company has grown rapidly
because of its management's and personnel's ability to
do their jobs well.

3. To help the reader understand immediately,
enumerate the main points of the message or present
them in outline form. Itemize things that lend
themselves to 1-2-3 listings.

4. Use headings, subheadings and side headings to
guide the reader. When you can, arrange material in
tables, charts, graphs, and lists.

HEADING STYLES.

Headings are used to indicate the organization of
material. Consistent headings help the reader to
understand organization and content.

Eight easy ways to make words work.

Eight easy ways to make words work.

One right word is worth a thousand pictures.

Nothing is so powerful as the right word at the right time.

On the other hand, nothing is so ineffective as the wrong word anytime.

A misspelled word; a redundant word; a word that's *close* to the word you really want, but isn't it; a word that's negative instead of positive; a word that's worn-out.

Review carefully these common word problems.

The more you work on words, the more words will work for you.

1. Two words aren't better than one.

For starters, avoid using two words with the same meaning. Simplify redundant expressions.

Will reduced doubletalk improve your persuasive powers?

You can say that again.

Doubletalk.	**Simplified.**
advance planning	planning
basic fundamentals	fundamentals
canceled out	canceled
city of Glendale	Glendale
close proximity	proximity
consensus of opinion	consensus
cooperate together	cooperate
deeds and actions	actions
depreciate in value	depreciate
final completion	completion
important essentials	essentials
month of December	December
necessary requirements	requirements
open up	open
over again	again
refer back	refer
rely and depend	depend
reason is because	reason is
repeat again	repeat
small in size	small
8 p.m. in the evening	8 p.m.
three weeks' time	three weeks

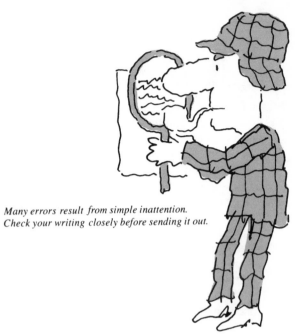

Many errors result from simple inattention.
Check your writing closely before sending it out.

2. How to choose a few well-chosen words.

Using the wrong word in a business situation can make you look like a business dunce.

Watch it. Be careful not to misuse or confuse words.

Here are a few of the most frequently confused words in English. Do you know the difference?

Affect means "to influence." (His attitude affected his work.)
Effect means "result." (The effect of these changes was good.)

Its is a possessive pronoun. (A computer has its own mind.)
It's is the contraction for *it has* or *it is.* (It's a severe problem.)

Your is a possessive pronoun. (Your problem has been solved.)
You're is the contraction for *you are.* (You're a wonderful secretary.)

Can implies ability. (Can you file this before noon?)
May denotes permission. (May I file it tomorrow?)

Imply means to "hint or suggest." (He implied that the report was incomplete.)
Infer means "to draw a conclusion." (We inferred that he wanted the report changed immediately.)

Capital can mean "of prime importance" or "money." (We have some capital to invest.)
Capitol means a "building in which a legislature meets."

Principal means "main or chief" (as in school principal) or "sum of money." (You can withdraw the interest, but not the principal.)
Principle refers to a rule or law. (Creating goodwill is a principle of good business.)

Anxious means "worried or fearful." (He was anxious about the cost of money.)
Eager means "enthusiastic." (We are eager to hear from you.)

Continually suggests interrupted action occurring over a period of time. (It will be necessary to monitor those accounts continually.)
Continuously indicates uninterrupted action. (The phones have been ringing continuously for one hour).

Lend is a verb meaning "to grant the use of something." (We can lend you the amount you requested.)

Loan is usually a noun meaning "temporary use of something." (We will be happy to approve your loan.)

A business writer's best friend is his dictionary.

3. It pays to be positive.

If you have a glass filled to the midpoint with water, is it half empty or half full?

Psychologists advise that if you present matters from a positive point of view, what you have to say will appear much more attractive to people.

Be positive—use words that convey a positive attitude wherever possible.

Here are some examples of the power of positive thinking.

Positive Words.	Negative Words.
advancement	you claim
satisfaction	your complaint
gratify	not entitled to
earnest	delayed
cheerful	fault
valued	uncertainty
liberal	mistake
sincerely	unfortunate
enjoy	you failed to
confident	bankrupt
welcome	neglect
progress	inconvenience
courage	must refuse
agreeable	we are sorry
success	careless
happy	oversight
easy	impossible
comfortable	we regret
pleasure	you forgot
fortunate	cannot
cordial	dispute
willing	unable
eager	company policy
attractive	not
trustworthy	
integrity	
encourage	
profit	
generously	

Here's one more positively invaluable suggestion—avoid using "if" where the word indicates a choice. Assume that your reader will respond positively.

Not: If you review our proposal,
                    we can discuss the agreement.

But: After you review our proposal,
                    we can discuss the agreement.

4. Make your numbers count.

WHEN TO USE WORDS AND WHEN TO USE NUMERALS.

You've got to watch out for numbers.

Unfortunately, some people just never get it straight when to write numbers using numerals, and when to express numbers with words.

USE NUMBERS CONSISTENTLY.

First, always try to use numbers consistently.

There are, in fact, a number of times you should always use *numerals* to represent numbers.

1. Always use numerals for easy comprehension and reference.

2. Always write sums of money in numerals. With even-sum numbers, you can omit the decimal point and two zeroes.

3. Always express periods of time mentioned with common financial terms, such as discount and interest rates, in numerals.

4. Always use numerals to *emphasize* numbers.

5. Always express percentages in numerals, followed by the word "percent." Use the percent symbol (%) mainly in tables, invoices, memos, and statistical and technical materials.

USE WORDS WHEN
NUMBERS ARE AWKWARD.

First, you should spell out the numbers 1-10 and multiples of 10 up to 100—like one, two, three...ten, twenty, thirty et cetera.

In general, you should spell out any number that can be written in one or two words—like sixteen or two million.

Don't let numbers overwhelm you. There's a way to handle any numerical situation once you know the basic rules.

Here are some other places words are the preferred way to express numbers:

1. *At the beginning.* Use words for numbers at the beginning of a sentence. If the number is very long, rewrite the sentence so that the number is not at the beginning.

2. *Fractions.* Use words to write a single fraction—one-fourth. Spell out a mixed number (a fraction and a whole number) only at the beginning of a sentence.

3. *Compound numbers.* Write the first of two numbers used as a compound modifier as a word, the second as a figure: twenty 15-cent stamps.

Don't forget to use a hyphen to join compound numbers and fractions—two-thirds salary, twenty-five shares.

As a general rule you should spell out any number that can be written in one or two words.

5. Divide and conquer.

When you divide a word in the wrong place, it always looks slightly strange. Worse, it isn't business-like.

Follow these twenty or so word-splitting rules, and you will avoid splitting headaches.

1. Divide words only between syllables: sec-tion, ser-vice.

2. Do not divide one-syllable words: thought, not thought.

3. Do not divide at a one-letter syllable at the beginning or end of a word: amount (NOT: a-mount), cri-teria (NOT: criteri-a).

4. Do not divide a word unless you can leave a syllable of at least three characters (including the hyphen) on the upper line, and carry a syllable of at least three characters (including punctuation) to the next line: al-most, there-fore.

5. Do not divide abbreviations: USC, FBI.

6. Do not divide contractions: don't, not do-n't.

7. Do not divide amounts of money written in figures: $724.39, not $724.-
39.

8. Divide only at the hyphens in a hyphenated word: long-term, not long-term.

9. Divide words after a one letter syllable: capi-tal.

10. Do not divide the last word on any more than two consecutive lines.
11. Divide dates at the comma: June 24, 1985.

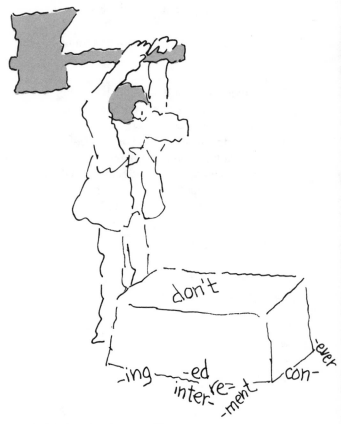

Think before chopping a word in two.
Don't divide contractions like don't.

12. Do not divide the last word in a paragraph or the last word on a page.

13. Do not divide words that have fewer than 6 letters: going, not going.

14. Divide between two one-letter syllables: punctuation.

15. Do not divide a person's last name: Williams, not Williams.

16. Divide after a prefix or before a suffix: in-complete, permis-sible.

17. Divide after the basic word in words ending in -ing: manag-ing, not ma-
naging.

18. Do not separate a number from the word "page": page 37, not page
37.

19. Do not separate a month and day, or a month and year: May 21, not May
21.

20. Do not separate a number and an abbreviation: 12:30 p.m., not 12:30
p.m.

6. Don't use cliches like "divide and conquer."

Unfortunately, cliches abound in business communication. Why make things even worse? Try to find fresh ways to express your ideas.

**Possibly the 12
worst business cliches.**

herculean effort
the worse for wear
clear as day
goes without saying
run it up the flagpole
abreast of the times
burning issues
piece of cake
ready and willing
see if it flies
lesson for us all
no sooner said...

7. Are you "spell" bound?

At all costs, avoid spelling mistakes. Business
people assume that if you can't spell, you can't think.
When in doubt, use the d-i-c-t-i-o-n-a-r-y or a
s-p-e-l-l-i-n-g g-u-i-d-e.

That's what they're for.

The following words are often misspelled.
Memorize just 25 every day. When you can correctly
spell them, you'll deserve an MBA in spelling.

absence	acquiesce	amateur
accidentally	acquire	amortize
accommodate	acquisition	analysis
accompanied	adjacent	analyze
accompanying	advantageous	apparatus
accumulate	aggravate	apparent
achievement	aisle	apologize
acknowledgment	alleged	appearance
acquaintance	all right	appetite

appreciable	catalog	criticism
approaching	category	curiosity
appropriate	changeable	dealt
approximately	chronological	decision
argument	coincidence	defendant
arrangement	collateral	defense
article	column	deficit
ascend	commemorate	definite
assistance	commitment	dependent
attendance	committee	descend
attorney	community	descendant
audience	comparative	desirable
auxiliary	comparison	despair
bankruptcy	compelled	desperate
basically	competition	destroy
beginning	concede	detrimental
believed	conceive	develop
beneficiary	conscience	dictionary
benefited	conscientious	different
biased	conscious	difficulty
boundary	consensus	dilemma
brilliant	continuous	disappear
bulletin	controversy	disappoint
campaign	convenience	disastrous
canceled	correspondence	discipline
candidate	courteous	dissatisfied

Don't hide behind big words.
Everyone knows you're there.

49

dissimilar	grateful	liaison
divided	grievous	license
doubt	guarantee	listen
efficiency	guard	livelihood
eighth	guardian	loneliness
eligible	helpfulness	maintenance
eliminate	hindrance	maneuver
embarrass	hoping	maybe
emphasize	humorous	meant
endeavor	hurriedly	mileage
entrance	illegible	miniature
enumerate	illiterate	minimum
environment	immediately	miscellaneous
equipped	inadequate	mischievous
especially	inasmuch as	misspell
exaggerated	incidentally	morale
excellent	incredible	mortgage
excitement	independent	naturally
exhausted	indispensable	necessary
exhibition	influence	negotiate
existence	innocuous	neither
exorbitant	innovation	nevertheless
explanation	insistence	nickel
extension	intelligence	ninety
facsimile	interesting	noticeable
fascinating	interfere	nowadays
February	interpreted	obstacle
finally	interrupted	occasionally
foresee	irrelevant	occurred
forfeit	irresistible	occurrence
forty	itinerary	offense
fourteen	judgment	omission
fourth	knowledge	omitted
fulfill	labeled	oneself
gauge	legible	operate
generally	leisure	opinion
government	liable	opportunity

optimistic	procedure	scarcely
original	proceed	schedule
outrageous	professional	seize
paid	programmed	sense
pamphlet	prominent	separate
parallel	psychology	serviceable
paralyzed	publicly	severely
partially	pursue	shining
particularly	quantity	similar
pastime	questionnaire	simultaneously
patience	queue	sincerely
peculiarity	quitting	skillful
permanent	quizzes	source
permissible	realize	specimen
perseverance	really	sponsor
persistent	reasonably	strength
personnel	receipt	strenuously
persuade	received	stretched
phase	recipient	strictly
phenomenon	recognize	studying
plausible	recommend	submit
pleasant	recruit	subpoena
possession	reference	subsequent
practically	referred	subtlety
precede	relevant	subtly
predecessor	relieve	succeed
preferable	religious	successful
preference	remembrance	suing
preferred	renowned	summary
prejudice	repetition	supersede
preparations	rescind	suppress
prerogative	resistance	surely
prescribe	resource	surprise
pretense	resume	surveillance
prevalent	ridiculous	susceptible
privilege	sacrifice	technique
probably	satisfactory	temperament

temperature	tremendous	variable
tempt	undoubtedly	varieties
therefore	unmanageable	vigorous
thoroughly	unnecessary	wholly
threshold	until	wield
transferring	usually	

*Get to the point! You can
often make your case more
quickly with one right word.*

8. Stop word smog.

Be specific. Avoid using fuzzy generalizations,
roundabout expressions and vague, abstract wording.

Don't hide behind big words.

Get to the point.

Concrete words are easy to understand, and a
clear word picture will help keep your reader's
attention.

Avoid using vague words like "it" or "there" to
begin a sentence. Stop "abstractitis" before it starts.

Abstract: There will soon be a slight rate increase.

Concrete: In three days, rates will increase one-
quarter percent.

How to succeed at grammar.

How to succeed at grammar.

Grammar can make you or break you.

Admittedly, grammar is one important aspect of good business writing that isn't glamorous.

At best, it's only grammarous.

Don't let that stop you.

Study these twelve rules of grammar, and you will come to discover that grammar is the business professional's best friend.

1. She versus her.

To determine which pronoun is correct in expressions like "Sue and she/her," read the sentence omitting the "and" and the noun or pronoun that precedes "and."

Sue and (*she*/her) went to the third floor.
(She went to the third floor.)

We sent Sue and (she/*her*) to the third floor.
(We sent her to the third floor.)

2. When to use who and whom.

To decide whether *who* or *whom* is correct, substitute *he* or *she; him* or *her.* When *he* or *she* is correct, use who. When *him* or *her* is correct, use whom.

Joe is the one (*who*, whom) can type 90 wpm.
He can type 90 wpm.

The customer (who, *whom*) you helped yesterday is calling.
You helped *him* yesterday.

3. It's wrong to be self-centered.

Pronouns ending in *self* or *selves* should only be used when they refer to a noun or pronoun that has already appeared in the sentence.

Wrong: Bob, Harry and *myself* answered the calls.
Correct:

> Bob, Harry and *I myself* answered the calls.
> Bob, Harry and *I* answered the calls.

4. Can we have some agreement here?

A pronoun should agree in number, person, and gender with the word to which it refers.

Examples: Every*one* should bring *his* (or *her*) book.
All employees should complete their work.

5. Numbers.

The indefinite pronouns *anybody, anyone, everybody, everyone, one, somebody, nobody, no one, each, either,* and *neither* are singular.

Not: *Everyone* should bring *their* lunch.
               (singular)   (plural)

But: *Everyone* should bring *his*
               (singular)   (singular)
               (or *her*, or *his or her*) lunch.

6. Various persons.

Don't forget. Pronouns come in several persons.

First Person: I, we.

Second Person: you.

Third Person: he, she, it, they.

Not: Unless a *person* knows exactly where
               (3rd person)
               to look, *you* should ask for help.
               (2nd person)

But: Unless a *person* knows exactly where
               (3rd person)
               to look, *he* should ask for help.
               (3rd person)

7. Remember gender.

When the gender of the antecedent (the word to which the pronoun refers) can be either masculine or feminine, use *he, him* and *his*.

You can use *he or she, him or her*, and *his or hers.* But when there are too many of these references, use the masculine forms.

Example:

Every student should bring his book.

8. Subject-verb agreement.

A subject must always agree with its verb in number. A singular subject demands a singular verb. A plural subject demands a plural verb. Please, no arguments on this one.

Be careful—modifying phrases and clauses that come between a subject and verb can cause confusion.

Do not let a noun that comes before the verb trick you. Keep the simple subject in mind.

Examples:

The *report* by the committee chairman
    (subject)
and the board members (*has*, have) been sent
to the printer.

Not *one* of the reports from the new
    (subject)
departments (*is*, are) ready yet.

The *reports*, as well as the booklet,
    (subject)
(has, *have*) to be finished this week.

9. Compound subjects.

A compound subject joined by "and" takes a plural verb.

The statistics and the computer information
    (compound subject)
(is, *are*) ready for careful review.
    (plural verb)

10. Or versus nor.

The words "or" and "nor" indicate a choice. When a compound subject is joined by "or" or "nor," the verb agrees with the part of the subject nearest to it.

Examples:

Neither he *nor she* (*is*, are) available this afternoon.

Before the summaries *or* the *report* (*is*, are) sent, we need to make copies.

(Is, *Are*) the *reports or* the statement to be mailed?

11. Collective nouns.

They may look singular in form, but collective nouns actually name a collection or group of things.

If you are thinking of the group as a whole or as a single unit, use a singular verb.

Example: The *committee* (*is*, are) meeting this
  Thursday.
   (the group as a whole)

If you are thinking of the individual members of the group, use a plural verb.

12. To each his own.

Each of the following words indicates one person or thing and takes a singular verb: *every, either, each, neither, everyone, everybody, anyone, anybody, somebody, someone, nobody, no one, anything, everything, many a, something, nothing, one, another.*

Example: Each of the letters (*was*, were) typed
  beautifully.

*Get smart. Breaking the rules of grammar
will never get you a corner office.*

To succeed in business, start as a great capitalist.

What should you capitalize, and what shouldn't you capitalize? Here are some capital suggestions:

• Capitalize each item in a list or outline.

• Capitalize the names of units within your organization when they are preceded by ''the'' —*The Marketing Division* in contrast to *our marketing department.*

• Do not capitalize terms that refer to units within another organization, unless you want to emphasize the terms or show special respect.

• Capitalize words like customer service and public relations only when they are used alone to designate a department within an organization.

Example: Please forward this request to Advertising or Public Relations.

• Capitalize all words in a title or displayed heading except the following: *the, a, an, and, as, but, if, or, not, at, by, for, in, of, off, on, out, to, up.*
Exception—capitalize any of the above at the beginning of a title or heading.

Correct:　　Home for Retired Fire Eaters
Also Correct: The Retired Fire Eaters' Home

• Capitalize a noun followed by a number or letter.

Example:　　Article 4, Check No. 242.

Exceptions—do not capitalize words including *line, note, page, paragraph, size.*

• Capitalize a title when it is used as part of a name.

Example:　　At the speech's conclusion, the audience gave Division Manager William Fuller a standing ovation.

　　　Under most other circumstances, do not capitalize titles unless they are those of very important government officials.

Examples:　　Please speak to our office manager.
Paul Johnson, our treasurer, will contact you.

The Queen has not returned your call.

Make your mark with punctuation.

Make your mark with punctuation.

You can't write without it, period.

Correct punctuation indicates a business writer who is decisive and in command.

Incorrect punctuation indicates a business writer who is in serious trouble.

Punctuate *correctly.*

Misplaced or missing punctuation can confuse your reader or cause him to misunderstand.

1. Punctuating independent clauses.

A main clause or independent clause is a complete sentence.

Example: We can process the forms.

However, several independent clauses can also be *combined* into a single sentence, using the following connective punctuation.

Punctuation: Comma and Conjunction (*and, but, or, nor, yet, for*).

Example: We can process the forms, *and*
                        (independent)
               you can notarize them.
                        (independent)

Punctuation: Semicolon and Conjunctive Adverb (used when sentences already contain commas).

Example: We ordered two typewriters, three desks and two chairs;
                        (independent)
               however, you sent us two desks and two typewriters.
                        (independent)

Punctuation: Semicolon (used when the ideas in the sentences are related).

Example: We can process the forms;
                        (independent)
               then you can notarize them.
                        (independent)

Punctuation: Semicolon and Transitional
Expression

Example: We can't process the forms;
nevertheless,
(independent)
you can notarize them.
(independent)

Punctuation: Dash (used to emphasize the second
part).

Example: We know we can trace the source of
(independent)
the error—everything is on tape.
(independent)

Punctuation: Colon (used when second independent
clause explains the first).

Example: We know we can trace the source of
the error:
(independent)
every transaction is recorded on tape.
(independent)

2. Punctuating dependent clauses.

A dependent clause is not a complete sentence. It depends on and is connected to a main (independent) clause to form a complete sentence.

Example: When you return the enclosed application,
(dependent clause)
we can process the forms.
(main or independent clause)

A dependent clause may occur before, within, or after a main clause.

Before: *If you are early*, you can relax before the program begins.

After: You can relax before the program, *if you are early.*

Within: You can, *if you are early*, relax before the program begins.

An essential dependent clause tells which particular thing or person is meant. It is necessary to the meaning and structure of the sentence. Commas are not used with an essential clause.

Example: We have noted the memo *which advises that we record the ABC files.*

A nonessential clause gives explanatory detail about a particular person or thing. It is not necessary to the basic meaning or structural completeness of the sentence. Use commas to set off a nonessential clause.

Example: We have noted your memo of January 14, *which advises that we record the ABC files on tape.*

"Of January 14" identifies the memo and the italicized clause only adds information about the memo.

Three dependable examples.

Punctuation: Comma (to set off a dependent clause at the beginning of a sentence).

Example: *If you read the report,* you can understand why Mr. Blofeld fired himself.

Punctuation: Comma (to set off a nonessential dependent clause).

Example: We have noted your memo of January 16, *which advises that we buy a new tape recorder.*

Punctuation: Dashes (to call special attention to a nonessential dependent clause).

Example: The first issue—*which was, as you know, lost*—turned up yesterday.

Subordinate conjunctions.

Subordinate conjunctions and relative pronouns introduce dependent clauses.

after	since
although	so that
as	that
as if	though
as soon as	till
as though	unless
because	until
before	when
even if	whenever
how	where
if	wherever
in case that	whether
in order that	while
provided that	why

Relative pronouns.

who	whom
which	that

3. Punctuation used in a series or list.

Punctuation: Comma (to separate three or more items).

Example: We need *paper, pencils,* and *reference sheets* for the seminar.

Punctuation: Comma (before "etc." in a series within a sentence).

Example: The pencils, paper, reference sheets, *etc.* have been sent.

Punctuation: Semicolon (used to separate elements in a series of items containing commas).

Example: Members of the committee included James Warner, president; Samuel Snyder, executive vice president; and Bud Berns, manager.

Punctuation: Colon (used to introduce a list which follows a complete sentence).

Example: Mr. Sampson demanded several things: an immediate monetary adjustment, a written apology, and a new timetable.

Punctuation:	Colon (used to introduce a list of appositives—nouns that explain or add information about another noun).
Example:	Three items are missing on the check: *the amount, the date and your signature.*
Punctuation:	Parentheses (used around letters or numbers that precede the individual items in a series or list within a sentence).
Example:	Please be sure to (1) send me a copy of the letter, (2) notify me when you have received the contract, and (3) sign and notarize the contract before our meeting.
Punctuation:	Periods (used after letters or numbers in an outline or displayed list unless they are enclosed in parentheses).

Example: I.
    A.
    B.
        1.
        2.
            a.
            b.
                (1)
                (2)
                    (a)
                    (b)
                        1)
                        2)

Punctuation: Periods (used after long phrases and clauses in a list—and after short phrases that are essential to the meaning of the sentence that introduces them).

Examples: Get a signature card from
1. George Sander.
2. Jackie Smith.
3. Ann Burns.
Please bring the following:
1. a pencil.
2. a pen.
3. a pad.

or

Don't forget
1. Bob;
2. Marie; and
3. Sam.

4. Punctuating adjectives.

Punctuation: Comma (used between two or more
               adjectives that modify the same
               noun—coordinate adjectives).

Example: It was a clear, *concise* report.
   Note – "and" sounds correct between coordinate
   adjectives, and coordinate adjectives can be
   reversed in order.

Punctuation: Comma (used to separate a series of
               adjectives from the rest of the sentence
               when they do not appear directly
               before the nouns or pronouns they
               modify).

Example: *Clear and concise,* the report was
               written beautifully.

Punctuation: Hyphen (used to connect two or more
              words to create a new concept).

Examples:

a number-coded system	(noun + participle)
a tax-free purchase	(noun + adjective)
a smooth-running machine	(adjective + participle)
a three-toed sloth	(adjective + noun + -ed)

5. Punctuating transitional expressions.

Punctuation: Comma (used to set off introductory transitional expressions).

Example: *Consequently,* we would like to meet with you before we take action.

Play your connectives right, and you've got punctuation in the palm of your hand.

Punctuation: Commas (used to set off transitional expressions that introduce a single word or phrase).

Example: Many mathematical errors, *for example,* transpositions, are easy to find.

Punctuation: Semicolon and Comma (semicolon before and comma after a transitional expression that introduces an independent clause).

Example: We can hire a professional in space planning; *for example,* we can hire someone who has worked in an architectural firm as a space planner.

Punctuation: Colon and Comma (colon before and comma after a transitional expression that introduces a series of words, phrases, or clauses at the end of an independent clause).

Example: Mr. Sampson demanded several things: an immediate monetary adjustment, a written apology, and a new monogrammed briefcase.

Some popular transitional expressions.

Contrast and comparison: by contrast, by the same token, conversely, instead, likewise, on one hand, on the contrary, on the other hand, rather, similarly, yet, but, in spite of this, besides.

To show exception to what has been said: anyway, at any rate, be that as it may, even so, however, in any case, in any event, nevertheless, still, this fact notwithstanding, but.

Sequence: afterward, at first, at the same time, finally, first, first of all, for now, for the time being, in conclusion, in the first place, in time, in turn, later on, meanwhile, next, second, then, hence, thus, to begin with, above all, after all, again, further, still, then, too, before, now, originally.

Diversion: by the by, by the way, incidentally.

To introduce examples: for example, for instance, for one thing, namely, that is.

Addition: also, accompanied by, as well as, besides, furthermore, in addition, moreover, plus, together with, too, what is more, further.

Cause and effect: accordingly, as a result, consequently, hence, otherwise, so, then, therefore, thus, for this reason, because of this.

Summarizing: after all, all in all, all things considered, briefly, by and large, in any case, in any event, in brief, in conclusion, in short, in summary, in the final analysis, in the long run, on balance, on the whole, to sum up, ultimately.

Generalizing: as a rule, as usual, for the most part, generally, generally speaking, in general, ordinarily, usually.

Restatement: in essence, in other words, namely, that is, that is to say.

Put your skills to the test.

Put your skills to the test.

Pass, and you're in business.

If you have read this book carefully and thoroughly, congratulations. You're on your way to bright new business writing success. But first, this final test.

Section I.
Correct these sentences:

Sometimes it's hard to take the business world seriously. Here are twelve classic examples:

1. I recommend that customer service representatives be enlarged to fill the growth caused by our expansion.

2. Being of straw, I do not think we can satisfactorily insure your house.

3. In order for us to complete the papers, we will need the birth certificate of your son, that you should include in the enclosed envelope.

4. I succinctly hope that the Company can help you again at some point in time.

5. If you refuse to rise my celery, I will acquit this job at once.

6. Allow this letter to tinder my resignation.

7. Not until everyone become orientated can they take part in our highly competative business.

8. You're letter contained several errors, especially in it's edition.

9. Since you represent the Company, wear appropriate cloths.

10. In reference to you're letter, we do not offer better terms to professional athletes.

11. I couldnt understand your letter because it was puncutated to bad.

12. Unles you return the certificates, several policemens will call upon you at there earliest leisure.

Section II.
True or False.

The following are rules for superior business writing:

True	False		
☐	☐	1.	Make each pronoun agree with its antecedent.
☐	☐	2.	Verbs have to agree with their subjects.
☐	☐	3.	Watch out for irregular verbs which have crept into our language.
☐	☐	4.	Don't ever use double negatives.
☐	☐	5.	A writer must not shift his or her point of view.
☐	☐	6.	Always use the correct pronoun case. Your reader deserves to understand your meaning without unclear or incorrect references.
☐	☐	7.	Don't use dangling participles.
☐	☐	8.	Use conjunctions as you should: to join clauses.
☐	☐	9.	Don't write run-on sentences. Punctuate your sentences correctly.
☐	☐	10.	In letters, themes, reports, memos, and articles,use commas to separate items in a series.
☐	☐	11.	Don't write sentence fragments. Write complete sentences only.
☐	☐	12.	Don't use abbreviations in formal writing, and don't over-use contractions.

☐ ☐ 13. Always use apostrophes correctly.
☐ ☐ 14. Always check to see if you have left out any words.
☐ ☐ 15. Never misspell either common or unusual words.
☐ ☐ 16. Don't invert normal word order.
☐ ☐ 17. Don't be redundant.
☐ ☐ 18. Always proofread carefully.
☐ ☐ 19. In professional and business communications, never use non-standard English.
☐ ☐ 20. Always avoid cliches. Find fresh ways to present your information.

You will find the answers to this test on page 86.
Good luck.

Test Answers.

Section I.

We *told* you not to take this section seriously. These twelve horrifying examples of gross business illiteracy have been provided entirely for your entertainment.

You really don't need the answers.

Do you?

Section II.

One of the most important skills in business is the ability to scan the content of any letter, memo or report upside down.

It is with that valuable training in mind that the answers to Section II are here presented.

SECTION II ANSWERS: (1) True, (2) True, (3) True, (4) Positively, (5) For sure, (6) True, (7) Very true, (8) Yes, (9) True, (10) True, (11) This is true, (12) True, (13) True, (14) Also true, (15) Absolutely, (16) True, (17) True, (18) How true, how true, (19) Indeed, (20) True.

What's your problem?

What's your problem?

This book is designed to change the way you think about business writing.

Read It. Study it. Memorize it. And the knowledge you need will be there when you need it.

But what if you also forget it?

Use this simple directory to locate emergency help.

Reports.

Word use.

Grammar.

Punctuation.

Notes.

Notes may be the most satisfying form of business communication there is.

A chance to impress *yourself.*

Use this space to jot down thoughts that can help you later.

But whatever you write, keep it brief, clear and organized.

Notes.

Notes.

Don't let business writing unnerve you.
Success is just around the corner.